Learning Points

Look at the pictures together and point to the words as you read them.

Encourage your child to talk about his/her truck, favourite programmes on television, favourite clothes…

Ask simple questions – what noise do planes make? When do we need to put our wellingtons on?

Play spot the colour. Every picture contains something yellow. Look for this together and for yellow things at home and outside.

Encourage your child to behave like a real reader and to read the book to you and to his/her teddies!

Acknowledgment
The publishers would like to thank Maureen Hallahan
for the hand lettering used in this book.

A catalogue record for this book is available
from the British Library

Published by Ladybird Books Ltd Loughborough Leicestershire UK
Ladybird Books Inc Auburn Maine 04210 USA

my first yellow
picture
book

illustrated by JOHN DILLOW

horse

plane

lemon

butterfly

strawberries

frog

egg

pram

penguin

wellingtons

bucket
and spade

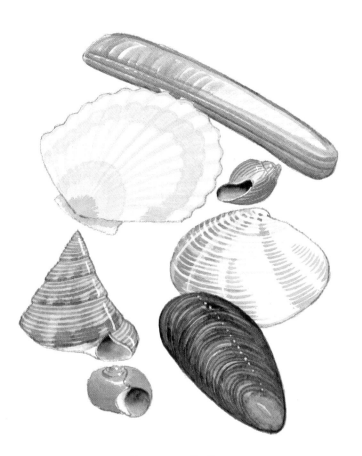

shells

truck

watch

television

mouse

plant

shirt

elephant

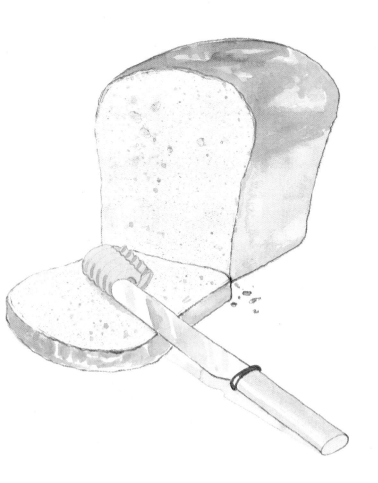

bread

flowers

crayons

camera

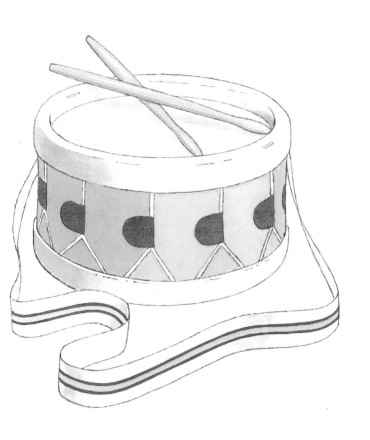

drum